Born to Die in My Place
A Timeless Story

Diana Rowe

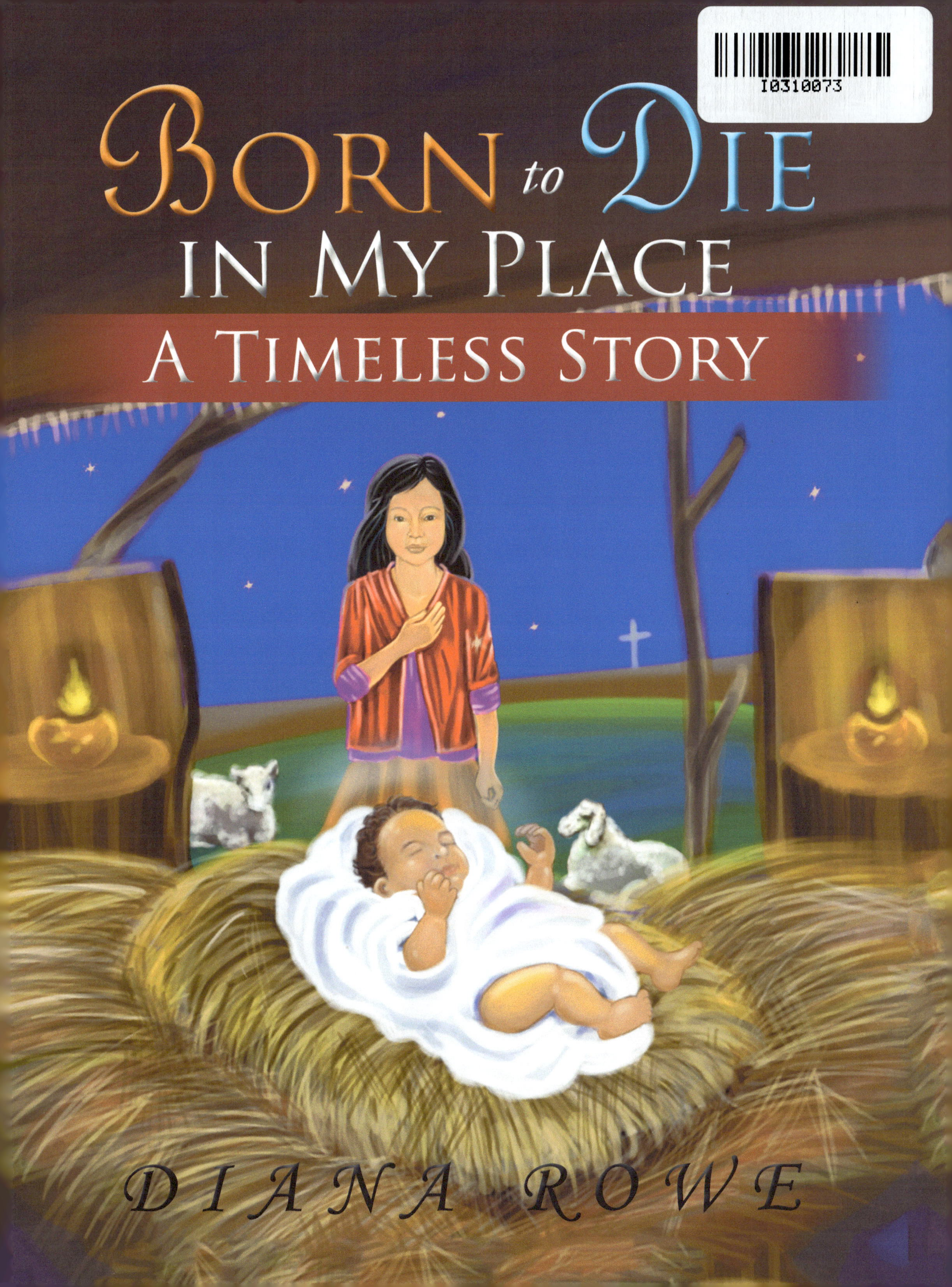

Copyright © 2014 by Diana Rowe.

Library of Congress Number: 2018909552

ISBN:
Paperback: 978-0-9989-4208-7
Hardcover: 978-0-9989-4209-4
EBook: 978-1-7326-9721-8

All rights reserved. No part of this book may be reproduced or transmitted in any form or by any means, electronic or mechanical, including photocopying, recording, or by any information storage and retrieval system, without permission in writing from the copyright owner.

Rev. date: 8/15/2018

Publisher: Lillie of the Vallie

Additional copies available at:
Lillieofthevallie.com

Dedication

This book is dedicated to my beloved mother Millicent and family. To my dear bro. Reynell Johnson whose kindness will never be forgotten.

Table of Contents

Dedication 1

A Special Holiday 5

Anna's Christmas 9

The Moments before the Miracle 12

A Savior for the Poor 16

A Savior for the Rich 18

A Priceless Gift 22

Show Appreciation for the Gift 26

Glossary 27

Before you begin

Do you have a favorite holiday?

What makes your holiday extra special to you?

A Special Holiday

People all around the world celebrate this special holiday every year. It is often hailed as "the happiest time of the year." It's the time of year when families get together to cook delicious meals and bake holiday cookies, cakes, and other delicacies dulcified with honey and enveloped in mouthwatering spices! These scents could drown your nose in a sea of scrumptiousness.

Even kindness seems to be very prevalent among strangers. You might find yourself holding the door for someone or sharing something you really like with a person you never met, far away in another country.

By now you might have guessed which holiday this might be.

There is something different in the atmosphere throughout this season. Sometimes, outside blooms a winter wonderland of sparkling snowflakes that gingerly touch your face.

At other times, joyful sounds interrupt the harsh cold air around your ears with melodious songs of Christmas! You'll hear words like "Joy to the world, the Lord is come" or songs like "Away in a Manger," "Silent Night," "O Little Town of Bethlehem," and many other favorites.

Then along the streets and in the malls, you can see the colorful lights twinkling everywhere, calling your eyes to look at the newest things.

Oh, don't forget the Christmas gifts! You know that's what Christmas is really all about, or is it? Yes! We will buy gifts for family and friends. As each day passes, we'll carefully wrap each one and place them under the Christmas tree dripping with an assortment of decorations, to be opened on Christmas Day.

"Splendid! This sounds like the perfect Christmas buzzing with abundance."

I can hardly wait to see what's in the boxes with my name on it. I like receiving gifts. That's my kind of Christmas, but Anna's Christmas is very different.

Anna's Christmas

My friend Anna celebrates the holiday with her grandma in a small town every year with the same old things from years gone by.

She lacked all the delicious foods, the fancy Christmas tree, and all the elaborate gifts.

Even so, Anna and Grandma never complained about the things they didn't have. Although they were very poor, Christmas was still very special to them.

Christmas was Anna's favorite time of the year. She loved to share unforgettable moments by the fireplace, listening to Grandma's Christmas stories.

On Christmas Eve, Grandma and Anna baked two small pies and warmed some apple cider before sitting by the little fireplace in the living room to stay warm.

Grandma often covered her shoulders with her special shawl, while Anna tried to get comfortable as she draped her legs with her cherished red blanket, in anticipation of Grandma's Christmas story. Grandma's hands shook as she picked up her tattered book and began to read.

Grandma's Story

The Moments before the Miracle

Thousands of years ago, "Caesar Augustus, a Roman Emperor, commanded that a census be taken. Every person in the entire Roman world had to go to his own town to register" (Luke 2:1).

Many people traveled from different places to register for the census in Bethlehem. The streets were filled with the noise of people hustling and bustling to find a place to stay. The inns were crowded with guests. It was first come, first served.

Among the travelers were Mary and Joseph, and they needed a place to stay. Can you imagine how exhausted they must have been? They traveled all the way from Nazareth to Bethlehem. Wouldn't you be tired after walking those long hours?

Perhaps some of the guests will give their room to Mary when they see that she is with child. Unfortunately, no one did.

With no room to spare, the innkeeper showed Mary and Joseph a shabby stable nearby where they could stay.

Joseph looked at Mary with sadness in his eyes, because he wished that he could take her to a lovely room with fresh, clean linens and a soft bed to rest her aching feet.

It was a tranquil night in the stable, though animals were all around. Mary knew it was time for her to give birth. So Joseph hastily gathered some straws and borrowed the animals' feeding trough to use as a bed for the baby.

Moments later, the long-awaited Messiah was born. His name was Jesus. Joseph wrapped Him in "swaddling clothes and laid Him in the manger" bed right next to His mother.

Mary was tired but overjoyed as she looked at His tiny hands and feet, stroked her fingers gently across His brows, and kissed His little cheeks. She wondered how her life and the rest of the world would be changed forever because of her baby.

All of heaven watched this great miracle. Then with sweet sounds, the angelic hosts echoed with a crescendo of joy throughout the vast halls of heaven: "Our Creator is born, the Savior, the Hope for all mankind!" This "glad tidings of great joy" must be delivered to those living on earth.

But who will be ready to hear this incredible news?

A Savior for the Poor

As time went by, visitors came to acknowledge and celebrate the birth of Jesus. The first group consisted of poor enthusiastic shepherds whose dark night was set aglow by angels who told them that "a Savior was born for you in the City of David, which is Christ the Lord" (Luke 2:11).

When the shepherds found Mary, Joseph, and Jesus in the stable, they rejoiced with them and told them about their amazing encounter with the angelic throng.

The shepherds were happy to know that a Savior was born to save them from their sins.

They really felt special, because the angels did say, "A Savior was born for you." Wow! Did you know that this same Savior was born for you and me? Oh yes! He is our Savior too!

Mary was happy to know that God shared the good news with these humble shepherds. The shepherds could not contain themselves because this was the best thing that ever happened to them.

So on their way home, they purposefully told every person they saw that the Messiah was born to save them from sin.

A Savior for the Rich

Finally, Mary and Joseph had another group of visitors. This time, their presence was graced by a group of rich, wise, exultant kings from the east, who were guided by God's star to the place where Jesus was in Bethlehem.

When the kings found Jesus, they knelt down and worshiped Him. Then they presented Him with "gold, frankincense, and myrrh" (Matt. 2:1–12).

These kings did not consider themselves too great to give honor to the Messiah, though His outward appearance had not displayed any signs of royalty whether in His clothing or surroundings. The wise men were moved by faith in God not by sight.

They accepted Jesus as God and gave Him their first gift: the gift of their hearts in worship.

Then they recognized that this baby was the King above all kings, so they gave their second gift: the gift of gold, which was "usually given to monarchs such as kings."

    These noblemen admitted that Jesus was a divine being; thus, they offered their third gift: the gift of frankincense, "which was burned during the worship to God."

    Lastly, the wise kings, who studied the word of God, accepted Jesus as the One who was born to die in their place. As a result, they offered their fourth gift: the gift of myrrh, "which was customary for use during burials."

    Jesus, who was only a baby, was also God, King, and Savior of the whole world.

A Priceless Gift

Glancing down at Anna, Grandma asked, "So, my dear Anna, what gift would you like to give to Jesus?"

Anna looked up at Grandma with confidence and said, "I can give Jesus my heart in my worship to Him. I really want to give Him my very best from everything that I have."

Grandma smiled with delight because Anna understood that Jesus deserves everything that she has, starting with her heart of worship.

While Grandma continued to read, Anna's mind was racing with thoughts about God's kindness to her. Grandma saw the look on her face and paused to invite Anna to share her thoughts.

Anna exclaimed, "I believe that God loves me so much that He was willing to be born even though He knew that He would have to die! I wish all the boys and girls and men and women would accept God's gift to the world!"

Jesus is the greatest gift!

After nodding in agreement with Anna, Grandma decided to share her favorite part of the Christmas story:

"I like the fact that God sent Jesus to those who are poor and to those who are rich.

So it doesn't matter if you're a humble little shepherd or a great king. Jesus loves you and was born to save you from all your sins. That's what Christmas is all about!

It's not about the amount of food you have or the gifts you receive or even the exact date of December twenty-fifth.

It's about the fact that Jesus was born on one of the three hundred sixty-five days in the year just to save me, and that deserves a celebration!"

Rejoice! For the baby king came down to the common manger to be lifted up on the cross "so that whosoever believes in Him should not perish, but have eternal life" (John 3:16, last part).

Ecstatically, Anna pulled herself from under her blanket and nestled her head on Grandma's lap, with her arms spread around her waist, and said, "Grandma, let's share the gift of Jesus this Christmas!"

"That's a brilliant idea," said Grandma. "We can start by sharing our pie and warm cider with our neighbors while you read them the Christmas story."

And off they went sharing the good news with their actions and their words until all the pie and cider was finished!

Merry Christmas to All Our Families and Friends around the World!

Show Appreciation for the Gift

1. What is one thing that you learned from this story that you are willing to share with someone right now?
_____
_____

2. How do you plan to celebrate Christmas after reading this book?
_____
_____

3. What gifts will you give Jesus this Christmas?
_____
_____

4. Who can you share this book with so that they can know about this awesome gift from God?
_____
_____

5. List five things you can do to show the love of Jesus this Christmas.
_____
_____
_____
_____

Glossary

This glossary contains definitions based on how they're used in this story. There might be other meanings for the words that are not included here.

anticipation:	Having expectation or hope
assortment:	A collection of different kinds of things
brilliant:	Exceptionally clever or talented
crescendo:	A gradual increase in loudness or intensity of music
delicacies:	A choice or expensive food
delight:	To feel happiness or joy
dulcified:	To sweeten
ecstatically:	To feel or express joyful excitement
elaborate:	Includes carefully arranged details in designing or planning
encounter:	An unexpected experience with someone or something
enthusiastic:	To have or show intense enjoyment
exhausted:	To be very tired
exultant:	Triumphantly happy
gingerly:	In a careful manner
hailed:	To approve happily or enthusiastically
prevalent:	Something that happens often at a particular time
scents:	A pleasant smell
swaddling cloth:	Pieces of cloth used to wrap a baby tightly
tranquil:	To be quiet or calm

www.ingramcontent.com/pod-product-compliance
Lightning Source LLC
Chambersburg PA
CBHW041438010526
44118CB00002B/113